Nursery Rhymes
for Troubled Times
a progressive poke in the eye

for
Outraged adults
of all ages

Copyright © 2020 by George Gilmer
Diddley-Dee Media

Library of Congress Cataloging Data available.

ISBN: 978-1-7351355-0-2 (pc)
ISBN: 978-1-7351355-1-9 (ebook)

All text, illustrations and book design
by George Gilmer

This book is available at special quantity discounts
for political and non-profit organizations, literary programs,
and other groups from Diddley-Dee Media.
Contact us at: georgietheporgie.com

Introduction

Nursery rhymes may seem like an unusual response to the chaotic political and social upheaval we find ourselves in today. Yet nursery rhymes—those quaint, singsong verses so many of us grew up hearing when we were young—have always been political.

Humpty Dumpty, Little Miss Muffet, Little Bo Peep, and hundreds of other rhyming ditties originating in France and the British Isles, have been passed along for generations both orally and in colorfully illustrated books as *The Mother Goose Nursery Rhymes.*

For us the old rhymes are whimsical. But in their day, the verses were thinly veiled commentary on corruption, power, injustice, and the social ills affecting the lives of real people. *Baa Baa Black Sheep* is actually about a medieval wool tax imposed in 13th century England. *Ring Around the Rosie* refers to the Great Plague of London in 1665. *Mary, Mary, Quite Contrary* concerns the rampant torture and murder of hundreds of subjects by the English Queen, Mary Tudor, also known as "Bloody Mary."

Nursery Rhymes for Troubled Times: A Progressive Poke in the Eye addresses many of the same themes plus current topics including race, gender, gun rights, political refugees and more. These verses place today's issues into an historical context while playfully illuminating the absurdities of our own tumultuous times.

After *Humpty Dumpty*, The Mother Goose Nursery Rhymes

Humpty Trumpty Wanted a Wall

Humpty Trumpty wanted a wall,
Humpty Trumpty promised us all:
"Our Mexican neighbors will fund it," he said.
They shrugged and retorted, "You're cracked in the head."

Humpty Trumpty Wanted a Wall
During the 2016 presidential campaign, candidate Donald Trump adopted the catchphrase *Build the wall* as a rallying point that was hugely successful with his supporters. Trump not only claimed that he would build a border wall between the U.S. and Mexico, but Mexico would actually foot the bill. The Mexican government responded emphatically that it would have nothing to do with funding a U.S.-Mexico border wall.

Rub a Dub Dub

Rub a dub dub
Three despots in a tub,
And who do you think they be?
The Butcher, the Shaker, the President-Maker—
Turn them out, knaves all three.

After *Rub a Dub Dub*, The Mother Goose Nursery Rhymes

Rub a Dub Dub
There has been an alarming increase in the number of authoritarian leaders during this decade. Three of the many political strongmen of our times include Kim Jong-un of North Korea, who assassinated members of his own family to consolidate power, Xi Jinping of China, who changed Chinese law to legally remain in power indefinitely, and Russia's Vladimir Putin, known for the military annexation of land from neighboring countries, as well as for sowing discord among western nations and interfering in their democratic elections.

Sing a Song of Mike Pence

Sing a song of Mike Pence,
Pockets full of wile.
Four and twenty sycophants
Lined up single file,
Waiting in the background
For the King to fall.
Isn't that a dainty dish
To set before us all?

The King was in his tower,
Counting out his money.
The Queen was in her penthouse,
Eating bread and honey.
Pence was in his church pew,
A smile upon his face,
Praying for his chance to put
Some women in their place.

After *Sing a Song of Sixpence,* The Mother Goose Nursery Rhymes

Ten Little Refugees

Ten little refugees
Standing in a line.
One died of hunger
And then there were nine.

Nine little refugees
Waiting at the gate.
Smugglers took their money
And then there were eight.

Eight little refugees
Fleeing Armageddon.
One took a bullet
And then there were seven.

Seven little refugees
Caught-up in conflicts.
One marched in protest
And then there were six.

Six little refugees
Trying to stay alive.
One was gang molested
And then there were five.

Five little refugees
Knocking at the door.
A border wall was put up
And then there were four.

Four little refugees
Trying to cross the sea.
The boat was overcrowded
And then there were three.

Three little refugees
With families just like you,
Banned for their religion
And then there were two.

Two little refugees
Encamped out in the sun.
One caught malaria
And then there was one.

One little refugee
Whose world became undone,
Tried to save her family,
And then there were none.

Ten Little Refugees
The world is in the midst of a global refugee crisis that continues to worsen. Currently over 70 million people around the planet have been forced from their homes because of conflict and persecution—the most in global history, and that number increases by 24 every *minute*. Of those, 26 million refugees have fled to other countries and more than half are children. In 2020 the U.S. took in the fewest number of refugees since Congress first created the nation's refugee resettlement program in 1980, even as the international crisis was ballooning.

After *Ten Little Indians,* traditional American verse

Why Did Colin Take a Knee?

Why did Rosa sit right down?
Why did Martin march through town?

Why did four at Woolworth's wait?
Why did Thurgood integrate?

Why did Malcolm raise a fist?
Why was Medgar's life at risk?

Why did Langston's poems ring?
Why did Maya's caged bird sing?

Why was Trayvon shot and killed?
Why was Laquan's lifeblood spilled?

Why can't everybody see
What made Colin take a knee?

Why Did Colin Take a Knee?
In 2016, professional football quarterback Colin Kaepernick began protesting racial oppression—specifically the numerous police shootings of African Americans—by kneeling during the National Anthem rather than standing. His protest was part of the Black Lives Matter movement sweeping the nation. Kaepernick was greatly maligned for his actions by many fans, politicians, and the football league, who claimed his protest was disrespectful to those in the military. His contract was not renewed, and no other NFL team would rehire him.

Hey Diddle Diddle

Hey diddle diddle
The cat and the fiddle
A gunman walked into the school.
The NRA laughed to see such sport
As my baby bled out in a pool.

After *Hey Diddle Diddle,* The Mother Goose Nursery Rhymes

Rudy Tootie

Rudy Tootie felt a duty
To become renowned.
He joined the circus for that purpose
As its favorite clown.

On TV he'd clown for free,
Dancing like a bear.
Such a cutie, snide and snooty,
Blowing off hot air.

Sing a Song of Mike Pence, Pg. 7

Vice President Mike Pence labels himself as a *born-again evangelical Catholic*. Pence has made it clear that his conservative religious beliefs guided his extremist positions on issues of gender throughout his career, including his stance on women in the workplace, abortion rights, LGBTQ rights, equal pay, and even his aversion to being alone in a room with any woman who is not his wife. While in Congress, Pence voted against equal pay for women three times.

Hey Diddle Diddle, pg. 12

Since a shooter massacred twenty first graders and six adults with an assault rifle at Sandy Hook Elementary School in 2012, there have been well over 400 students shot in more than 150 school shootings, and the numbers are growing steadily. The National Rifle Association, which has spent over $200 million since 1998 on political contributions, lobbying and advertising, continues to use its clout to discourage changes in gun laws that would make schools safer for children.

Rudy Tootie, pg. 13

Rudy Giuliani, former Mayor of New York City, became a personal attorney to President Trump in April of 2018. Within days, Giuliani was appearing on TV defending Mr. Trump's nefarious actions under investigation in the ongoing Russia Probe and the President's $130,000 payoff to porn star Stormy Daniels. Giuliani's bumbling appearances, and later the role he played in attempting to sway Ukrainian leaders to interfere in U.S. elections, led many Americans to wonder if the once-beloved mayor had become mentally unhinged.

Jack and Jill in the Me Too Era, pg. 15

The Me Too (or #MeToo) movement is a worldwide grassroots campaign waged against sexual harassment and assault. Me Too sprang up organically when movie mogul Harvey Weinstein was accused by numerous women in the film industry of decades of harassment and rape. The Me Too movement has encouraged and empowered women to speak out about their experiences with sexual harassment and sexual assault, confront perpetrators, and begin to change the culture of sexual violence that has plagued women for centuries in the U.S. and around the globe.

Little Bob Mueller, pg. 16

An investigation into Russian election interference and suspicious connections between the Trump campaign and Russian officials was conducted by Special Counsel Robert Mueller from May 2017 to March 2019. Millions of democrats eagerly awaited the results of the investigation, hoping proof of wrongdoing by the president would be exposed. Mueller presented his findings to the Attorney General, William Barr, who publicly released the 448 page report with heavy redactions, obscuring the findings and further frustrating Americans on the left.

There Was No Collusion, pg. 17

The phrase *There was no collusion!* was spouted hundreds of times by President Trump as the nation awaited the findings of Robert Mueller, the Special Council investigating Russian interference in the 2016 presidential election. Mueller made clear that although his office would not charge the president with a crime, neither did his findings exonerate President Trump, who appeared to have an unusually chummy relationship with the Russian President Vladimir Putin.

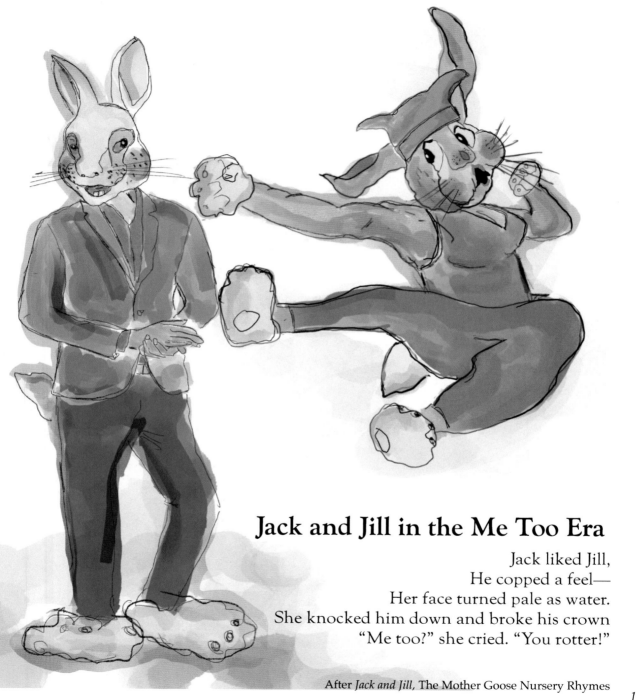

Jack and Jill in the Me Too Era

Jack liked Jill,
He copped a feel—
Her face turned pale as water.
She knocked him down and broke his crown
"Me too?" she cried. "You rotter!"

After Jack and Jill, The Mother Goose Nursery Rhymes

Little Bob Mueller

Little Bob Mueller
Come blow your horn!
There's sleaze in the meadow,
Moscow's in the corn.
Where is the boy who compiled all the facts?
He's let Barr bamboozle us with his redacts!

After *Little Boy Blue,* the Mother Goose Nursery Rhymes

There Was No Collusion!

Collusion?
Collusion?
There was no collusion.
Although no one
    believes it,
Mueller says it's so.

Delusion?
Delusion?
It's all a grand illusion.
Now let's all dance
    the *troika*,
And comrades, *let it go!*

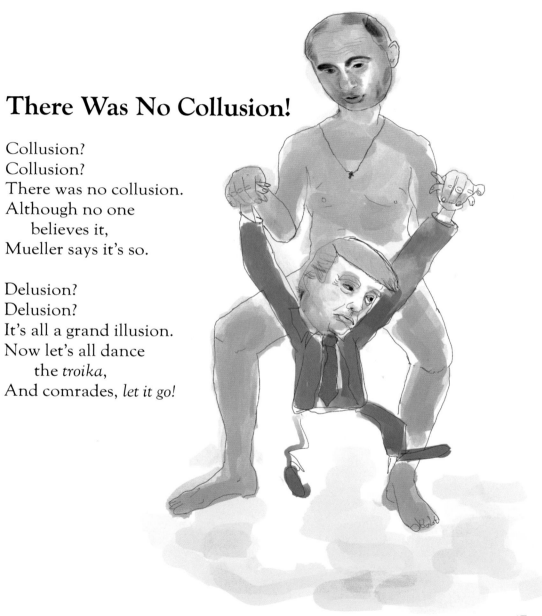

Building Blocks

Barack Obama really liked his blocks,
He built a tower of 'em in his socks.

Stacked a better healthcare—A.C.A.
Propped a weak economy up along the way.

Joined the World Agreement on Climate Change,
Blocked the Keystone Pipeline on the northern range.

Negotiated Trans-Pacific Partnership,
Placed a new Iran deal on the very tip.

Little Donny Trumpy came along to see,
Kicked the tower over—one, two, three!

Building Blocks
After eight years in the White House, President Barack Obama left a plethora of progressive policies, agreements, and laws in place. As Obama's successor, Donald Trump worked diligently to dismantle the Obama Legacy, seemingly out of sheer spite—including the dissolution of the Federal Pandemic Response Team put in place to protect Americans from outbreaks such as the COVID-19 Pandemic of 2020. One theory about Trump's unmitigated animosity towards Obama dates back to the 2011 White House Correspondents' Dinner in which President Obama publicly lampooned Trump's racist theories and political qualifications.

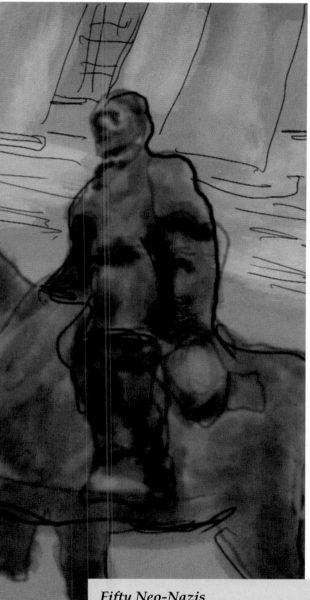

Fifty Neo-Nazis

Fifty neo-Nazis
All dressed in white
Went down to the monument
To start a little fight.

They brought some tiki torches
And chanted, "We're supreme!
We're Caucasian, we're self-righteous,
And our ideas are extreme.

"We love religious freedom
So we burn some churches down.
We lynch our frightened neighbors
'Cause their skin is mighty brown.

"Perhaps we're not as clever
Or as talented as some,
But we feel that we're entitled
Since we freckle in the sun."

The president was happy,
He said, "Nazis are alright—
Supremacist lives matter too,
You're special 'cause you're white."

Fifty Neo-Nazis
In 2017, a Unite the Right rally took place in Charlottesville, VA to protest the proposed removal of a Confederate statue. Ku Klux Klan members, neo-Nazis, and white supremacist groups converged with torches, semi-automatic weapons, Nazi symbols, and Confederate flags, chanting racist and anti-Semitic slogans. The event became violent as they clashed with counter-protestors. One self-identified white supremacist deliberately rammed his car into a crowd of counter-protesters nearby, injuring 40 people and killing one woman, Heather Heyer. President Trump was subsequently criticized for his comments in support of the hate groups.

This Little Piggy Had Opioids

This little piggy had opioids,
This little piggy had none.
This little piggy used heroine,
This little piggy wanted some.
This little piggy went *wee wee wee!*
All the way gone.

This little piggy made the pain meds
That this little piggy paid for.
This little piggy knew addiction
Would make Pharma profits soar.
This little piggy went *wee wee wee!*
All the way gone.

This little piggy had lawyers.
This little piggy had none.
This little piggy wanted answers,
This little piggy kept mum.
This little piggy went *wee wee wee!*
All the way gone.

After *This Little Piggy Went to Market*, The Mother Goose Nursery Rhymes

This Little Piggy Had Opioids
In 2019, the National Institute of Health reported that more than 130 Americans die every day from opioid abuse. Purdue Pharma, which developed and marketed the highly addictive opioid painkiller, OxyContin, was recently charged with multiple lawsuits, misbranding the drug as a less addictive opiate pain killer in a campaign to increase their profits, knowing all the while of the drug's highly addictive properties and the likelihood of untold numbers of deaths.

I Love Little Pussy

I love little pussy,
She's so fun to grab,
And if I don't fire her,
She prob'ly won't blab.
So I'll not ask her first,
I'll just grope her and smirk,
And pussy and I
Will play Chauvinist Jerk.

After *I Love Little Pussy*, The Mother Goose Nursery Rhymes

I Love Little Pussy
During the 2016 presidential campaign, a video released by *The Washington Post* exposed then-candidate Donald Trump discussing women with TV host Billy Bush saying, "You know I'm automatically attracted to beautiful—I just start kissing them. It's like a magnet. Just kiss. I don't even wait. And when you're a star, they let you do it. You can do anything. Grab 'em by the pussy. You can do anything." While many thought the ensuing public outcry would be the undoing of his chances for election, Trump's remarks were quickly rationalized as *normal locker-room banter*.

The Ballad of Covid Kid

Covid Kid pranced into town,
He'd come to gun the virus down
Without a clue of what to do—
He claimed it was a minor flu:
"This liberal hoax won't hurt you folks
With Covid Kid around."

"This sickness ain't so bad," he said,
Then he sat back and watched it spread.
"Nobody fret, I've placed my bet—
A miracle will happen yet!"
So he ignored as science roared,
And hundreds soon were dead.

The Governors were left alone
To stop the virus on their own,
And healthcare staff approached the task
Without the proper gowns or masks—
While Covid Kid so little did,
Yet glibly boasted on.

The markets fell and jobs were lost
As folks stayed home and paid the cost.
With steely nerve, resolve and verve
To flatten COVID 19's curve,
They hunkered down in every town—
As thousands more were lost.

Said Covid Kid, "I know this game,
I'll make somebody take the blame."
He picked someone Obama'd hired,
Then drew his gun and yelled, "You're fired!"
(T'was all that he knew how to do—
Let's face it, it was lame.)

The heroes of our woeful tale
Are citizens from every vale,
The nurses, docs, and science jocks
Who battled COVID 'round the clock,
And common workers laboring
In the face of Hell.

So ends the tale of Covid Kid
Who wore his ego on his bib.
Though he was brash and bold and tall,
He wasn't qualified at all—
And when he left, none were bereft
For all the good he'd did.

The Ballad of Covid Kid

When the COVID-19 coronavirus became a worldwide pandemic in the spring of 2020, President Trump—ignoring the expertise of his own team—claimed the virus was a democratic hoax that would quickly go away on its own "like a miracle." As the pandemic spread, he resorted to blaming others for the government's tepid response, including the nation of China, the World Health Organization, and even former president Barack Obama. In April of 2020, Trump fired Rick Bright, Director of the Biomedical Advanced Research and Development Authority and one of the world's leading experts in the field of infectious disease, for making public the fact that the U.S. was grossly unprepared for the virus and for calling on the federal government to rely on data when making scientific decisions during the pandemic.

Baa Baa Breitbart

Baa Baa Breitbart
Have you any bull?
Yes sir, yes sir, three blogs full.
One for conspiracists,
One for the alt-right,
And one for the tripe we spread
To foment scary shite.

After *Baa Baa Black Sheep*, The Mother Goose Nursery Rhymes

Baa Baa Breitbart

Breitbart News, founded in 2007, is known for content which has been called misogynistic, xenophobic, and racist by liberals and conservatives alike. The site has knowingly published a host of lies, conspiracy theories, and intentionally misleading stories to rally white supremacists, sow fear of immigrants and Muslims, and engender hatred towards progressive political leaders. Brietbart reached its zenith during the 2016 election cycle under Steve Bannon who labeled the site *The Platform for the Alt-Right* and who served for seven months in the White House as Donald Trump's chief strategist.

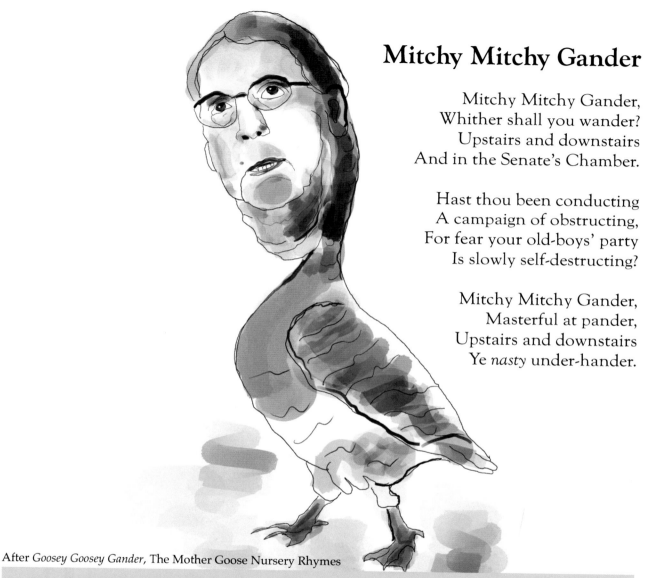

Mitchy Mitchy Gander

Mitchy Mitchy Gander,
Whither shall you wander?
Upstairs and downstairs
And in the Senate's Chamber.

Hast thou been conducting
A campaign of obstructing,
For fear your old-boys' party
Is slowly self-destructing?

Mitchy Mitchy Gander,
Masterful at pander,
Upstairs and downstairs
Ye *nasty* under-hander.

After *Goosey Goosey Gander*, The Mother Goose Nursery Rhymes

Mitchy Mitchy Gander

Senator Mitch McConnell, the leading republican senator from 2006-2020, is widely considered one of the greatest obstructionists in modern political history. After openly vowing to block any and all legislation put forth by the Obama administration over eight years, including even *considering* the confirmation of dozens of federal judges and a Supreme Court Justice, McConnell blocked hundreds of bills passed by the House of Representatives simply by declining to bring them to the Senate floor for debate. In 2020 McConnell brazenly obstructed the impeachment trial of Donald Trump to protect his party's control of the White House and Senate.

Ravenous Wolves are Lurking

In a forest dark and old
Of ancient groves and silver streams,
Wolves there lurk, so I've been told,
In the shadows deep and green.
Lads lured in to mystic wonder
Stroll among the fern and leaf—
Ravenous wolves there stalk and eat them,
Shred their lives with flashing teeth.

In cathedrals leafed with gold,
Of glowing glass and sacred verse,
Priests there lurk, so I've been told,
Behind the altar of the Church.
Lads are lured in holy wonder,
Family, custom, honor, trust—
Ravenous Priests there stalk and rape them,
Shred their lives and keep it hushed.

In a practice centuries old,
Of perverse acts and Christian shame,
Pedophiles lurk, so I've been told,
Protected by the Church's name.
Just *defrock* them? Give them prison!
The altered boys have borne such pain—
Ravenous secrets stalk and eat them,
Haunt their lives, forever maimed.

Ravenous Wolves Are Lurking

In 2002, an investigation by *The Boston Globe* led to widespread media coverage of decades of rampant sexual abuse within the Catholic Church, as well as the Church's pattern of covering up—and tacitly condoning—rape and pedophilia. Seventeen years later, at the conclusion of the 2019 meeting on the Protection of Minors in the Church, Pope Francis named pedophile priests "ravenous wolves," referencing a Biblical passage which reads, "Beware of false prophets, who come to you in sheep's clothing, but inwardly are ravenous wolves."

Planet on Fire, pg. 31

The indisputable fact that the earth's temperature is rapidly rising due to human activity continues to be largely ignored. Climate activist Greta Thunberg at the World Economic Forum in 2019 pleaded, "Adults keep saying: 'We owe it to the young people to give them hope.' But I don't want your hope. I don't want you to be hopeful. I want you to *panic*. I want you to *feel* the fear I feel every day. And then I want you to *act*. I want you to act as you would in a crisis. I want you to act as if our house is on fire. Because it is!"

Let's Have Open Carry Laws, pg. 33

A ten-year Assault Weapons Ban that expired in 2004 once prohibited the manufacture and sale of assault weapons and large-capacity munitions magazines to civilians. Research shows restrictions on these weapons would help prevent mass shooting injuries and deaths, as well as reduce the levels of horror associated with daily gun violence in America. Instead, gun enthusiasts and the NRA have argued that the weapons are needed for self-defense and for hunting, often touting the argument that *guns don't kill people—people kill people.* The fact is, both do, but people kill more people with assault weapons than without. To date, the ban has not been renewed.

The People in my Bubble, pg. 34

While the media Americans consume *may* provide accurate, informative news, it is also likely limiting our view-points with narratives that feed into our own confirmation biases, reinforcing what we already believe or agree with. In addition, the people we associate with—our friends, families, culture groups, work colleagues, places of worship and the like—are prone to reinforce our beliefs and world views, whether they are in fact correct or not.

I'll Make America Grate Again, pg. 38

Make America Great Again, the slogan for the 2016 Trump Campaign, became a rallying point for Trump supporters who often sported red MAGA caps at Trump rallies and elsewhere. As the nation became more politically polarized during Trump's tenure, the MAGA message was often seen as either unifying or divisive, depending on one's political affiliation. To many on the left, President Trump became increasingly abhorrent over time, until just the sight of a red MAGA cap grated the nerves.

The Pied Piper of Zuckerberg, pg. 44

The social media behemoth Facebook continues to be the most utilized tool on the planet in the spread of misinformation for fake news developers and unscrupulous political operatives. Facebook has stated that unless there is the prospect of real imminent harm, the company will continue to allow what founder Mark Zuckerberg calls the "widest possible aperture" for freedom of expression on the internet, insisting that it is up to its users to *decide* what is true or false. There are currently 2.45 billion Facebook users worldwide.

Thirsty in Flint, pg. 45

In 2014, the city of Flint, Michigan switched its public water source from Lake Huron to the Flint River in order to save money. When residents reported changes to the water's color, smell and taste, it was discovered that the polluted river caused high levels of toxic lead to leach into the water, as well as coliform bacteria, and trihalomethane chemical compounds. State and federal officials repeatedly denied that there was any issue with the water, manipulated test results, downplayed the problem, and lied to residents, who were predominantly poor and black. While the water is considered safe to use in 2020, many residents unsurprisingly remain skeptical.

Planet on Fire

Ladybug! Ladybug!
Fly away home.
The planet's on fire
And your children all gone.

The thrushes are thirsty,
The farms have turned brown.
The ice caps are wilting,
The reservoir's down.

Confused are the seasons,
Bemused are the bees,
Lost are the monarchs,
Aggrieved are the trees.

Yet partisans, petty
And little concerned,
Still posture, still falter,
Still quibble and spurn.

Ladybug! Ladybug!
Fly away home.
The planet's on fire
And your children all gone.

After Ladybug! Ladybug! Fly Away Home, The Mother Goose Nursery Rhymes

Swallowed by a Troll

I was swallowed by a troll today.
I went to my website with something to say,
When some unknown monster popped up like a fiend
And battered my dignity
Hanged my religion
Chewed my opinions
Gnawed on my gender
Stabbed my ethnicity
Kicked my intelligence
Spat on my family
And downed my esteem.
Have a nice day!

Swallowed by a Troll

Internet trolls are known for fomenting discord and starting online quarrels by posting inflammatory messages across cyber platforms. Over the past few years, trolling has evolved into an extreme form of personal harassment—attacking not just ideas and positions, but the people who post content online. Trolls instill anxiety, anger, shame, rage and fear. According to the Pew Research Center, Trolls find it is easy to stay anonymous as they harass and bully other people online, while it is difficult for platforms to design systems to stop them.

Let's Have Open Carry Laws
for shoulder-launch bazookas

Let's have open carry laws
For shoulder-launch bazookas,
So I can brandish one about
In case I have to shoot ya.

I'll look real tough for chicks and stuff.
In grocery stores I'll talk so gruff
I'll scare the wimpy little duffs
Who vote for liberal powder puffs.

I'll only launch in self-defense,
In case somebody makes me tense—
Like children playing near a fence,
Or hoodied lads... or darker gents.

I don't think it's a major deal,
At least this is the way I feel:
It's really not *bazooks* that kill,
It's just those *crazy people*.

So let's have open carry rules
For citizens (and common fools)
Who use bazooks as hunting tools—
It only makes good sense to.

The People in My Bubble

The earth, my friend, is flat.
It's actually flat—
The people in my bubble all agree.
Though science says it's round
I am looking at the ground,
And the place is just as level as can be.

Aliens are awesome.
They're absolutely awesome—
The people in my bubble all agree.
When they travel through deep space
To explore the human race,
I just know they'll come to earth
to study *me!*

Solar farms cause cancer.
They really do cause cancer—
The people in my bubble all agree.
Some think it's just a rumor,
But my Grandma had a tumor,
Which indicates a mass conspiracy.

Climate change is phony.
It's absolutely phony—
The people in my bubble all agree.
Sure, animals are dying
And the population's frying,
But last winter it got nippy as could be.

America is special.
We're just so very special—
The people in my bubble all agree.
So I favor costly healthcare,
And scoff at social welfare,
Which is why I live at
Mama's house for free.

Evolution is a theory.
It's no more than a theory—
The people in my bubble all agree.
Since nothing's ever new
In my narrow worldly view,
My beliefs have not evolved as you can see.

Inoculate the Nation

Polio was not so bad, I'm thinking—
It only killed some hordes and maimed the rest.
And smallpox wasn't large at all, I'll wager,
Except to those who caught it, I would guess.
And measles seem so measly, let me tell you,
Just tiny spots, mortality, and flu.
Inoculate a nation full of people?
Don't scientists have better things to do?

Inoculate the Nation
An anti-vaccination movement has been growing in the U.S. leading to outbreaks of diseases once thought to be eradicated or extremely rare. Measles, mumps, polio, rubella, and whooping cough are all on the rise due to anti-vaxxers choosing not to inoculate their children, believing the vaccines to be potentially more harmful than the diseases. Ironically, parents who refuse vaccines are most likely to be white, college-educated, and to have higher-than-average family incomes.

Urban and Rural Got Into a Fight

The term *Russian Interference* refers to ongoing covert efforts by the Russian government to sow discord, foment polarization, and influence elections in the United States and other countries. Although these attacks date back to Cold War days, Russia's efforts under Vladimir Putin became much more effective with the rise of social media, and there is no doubt the U.S. is more polarized today than it has been for many generations.

Urban and Rural
Got Into a Fight

Urban and Rural got into a fight,
They climbed in the ring
one Saturday night
To hound each other,
Pound each other,
Confound each other
In a battle of spite.

Urban struck the first Twitter slur,
Rural retorted
With thumbs ablur.
"You backwards hick!"
"You socialist prick!"
"You make me sick,
You lowlife cur!"

Rural swung right with a Fox News jab,
Urban counter-Times'd
An erudite dab.
"Un-American wimp!"
"Undereducated gimp!"
"I'll make you limp,
With your fake news blab!"

Urban was packing a concealed handgun,
Rural open-carried,
Which was way more fun.
They were talking tough,
They had had enough.
"I'm calling your bluff!"
"Your days are done!"

The American crowd was angry and hootin'
While there in the back
Sat Vladimir Putin.
He'd sown discord
Among the horde
And was looking forward
To an all-out shootin'.

The government said, "We'll referee,
Just vote it out—
It's Democracy!"
But Putin had tampered,
The elections were hampered.
The president, pampered,
Did diddley-dee.

Urban and Rural, standing toe-to-toe,
Couldn't find a way
To let it go.
Urban felt slighted,
Rural, uninvited.
Putin was delighted
With the whole shitshow.

I'll Make America Grate Again

I'll make America *grate* again,
On everybody's nerves.
I'll pass obnoxious policies
And then throw in a curve.
I'll do my best to give the people
Less than they deserve,
And make the nation grate again
On *everybody's* nerves.

Jeremy Mander, *Gerrymandered*

Jeremy Mander,
Jeremy Mander,
Whose box will you tick
Next election?
And do you suppose
The scoundrel who wins
Will represent voter complexion?

Jeremy Mander,
Jeremy Mander,
The lines they've drawn up
Are corrupted—
Your district meanders
All over the state,
For incumbency, uninterrupted.

Jeremy Mander, *Gerrymandered*

Gerrymandering—the process by which a political party establishes unfair voting districts in order to keep itself in power—is undermining our basic democracy. While both parties have used gerrymandering, there are currently more Republican-held states maintaining their seats through gerrymandering due to a well-organized national effort by conservative think tanks following the 2010 elections. In 2019, the Supreme Court ruled in a 5-4 decision that the Federal Courts *cannot* rule on gerrymandering, a move that has been widely viewed as a colossal Supreme Court cop-out.

The Caravan's Coming!

Listen, my children, and you shall hear
Of the midnight tweets of a bold racketeer,
Who saved our land from a mighty invasion
By some Honduran folk of the browner persuasion.

At the Rio Grande deep in the night
Near the north watchtower, just out of sight,
He said to his friend, "If the Caravan march
Hang a lantern aloft in the old belfry arch—

"One if by land, and two if by sea
And I in my ovally office will be,
Waiting with Twitter to spread the alarm
For the white country-folk to be up and to arm."

Onward the Caravan trudged day-by-day—
They were tired, they were poor, and they knew not the way.
Women and babies and children and men
Walked on with the hope they would be welcomed in.

In the hour of darkness and peril and need
To the hurrying tap-taps of that Twitter feed,
The people awakened to sit up and hear
The midnight spread of Caucasian fear:

"The Caravan's coming!"
"The Caravan's coming!"
"The Caravan's coming!"
"The Caravan's coming!"

After *Paul Revere's Ride* by Henry Wadsworth Longfellow

The Caravan's Coming!
In the months leading up to the 2018 midterm elections, President Trump and many republican lawmakers launched a vast media attack on a caravan of 7,000 impoverished Central American migrants who were walking to the U.S.-Mexico border to escape violence and economic hardship, casting the refugees as an invading army bringing crime, terrorism, and disease to the U.S. The ploy was designed to frighten Americans and galvanize support for republican candidates. The effort failed, however—democrats gained a large majority in the House of Representatives and turned six state legislative bodies and seven governorships blue.

Be Sure To Bring Your Pony

Susie brought a puppy,
Billy brought a cat,
Eric brought a possum in a porkpie hat.

Judy brought a rooster,
She led it on a strap,
And they all took them on a plane and held them in their laps.

I was feeling nervous
So I bought a fancy fox,
And took it on the airplane in a cardboard box.

The passengers were happy,
They didn't say a word.
No one thought support beasts were the slightest bit absurd.

So if you're going to travel,
For emotional support—
Be sure to bring your pony to the Air-O-Port.

Be Sure to Bring Your Pony
Every year in the U.S., thousands of animals including dogs, cats, birds, turkeys, pigs, snakes, turtles, fish, monkeys, and even ponies are brought on domestic flights as emotional support animals. There have been many incidents involving mauling, biting, growling, pooping, barking, hissing and the like. Most airlines have tightened their requirements for bringing along support animals. Delta Airlines recently expanded its list of prohibited animals to include "farm poultry, hedgehogs and anything with tusks."

Be Part of the Problem

Tweet every single
Uncouth thought
That flutters
Through your mind.

Pontificate,
Exacerbate,
Don't check the facts—
Tweet blind!

Be arrogant,
A know-it-all,
Perpetuate
Some vitriol.

No need to shout,
Just Tweet it out,
And be part of

The problem.

Be Part of the Problem
For better or worse, Twitter has become a ubiquitous part of the social, political, and media landscape in the U.S. Politicians, media outlets, celebrities and ordinary citizens post millions of Tweets each day in response to news, events, and other Tweets. Although Twitter posts may be innocuous, in many instances Tweets serve to vilify, disparage others, and spread falsehoods. The terms *Twitter War* and *Twitter Feud* have become part of the common lexicon. Donald Trump became infamous for his regular use of vitriolic Tweets while in office.

The Pied Piper of Zuckerberg

The notes he played
floated sweetly—
We danced as we followed along.
We forgot about caution completely,
Never questioning
what could go wrong.

After *The Pied Piper of Hamelin*, traditional German folktale

Thirsty in Flint

Water, water, everywhere,
And not a drop to drink.
The tap at home spews poison out
Into the kitchen sink.

Nobody wants to take the blame
'Bout how the funds were spent,
But politicians wrecked our lives
When they helped out in Flint.

After *The Rime of the Ancient Mariner,* by Samuel Taylor Coleridge

Paradise is Burning

Paradise is burning—
The world we've come to know,
Where trees of pine have weathered time,
Where owls take wing in woods sublime.
Now forest-bound Sequoias glow
Through winter-weighted boughs of snow.
We've loved our homes among the grow,
But Paradise is burning.

Paradise is burning—
The men search for their wives
Upon the grounds of homes burned down.
A distant blaze the only sound
Like angry bees in humming hives,
The fire consumes and grows and thrives.
So many souls have lost their lives
Since Paradise is burning.

Paradise is burning—
The die has now been cast.
Monoxide chokes our eyes and throats
And eats the planet's mighty oaks.
We burned our fossil fuels too fast
And told ourselves the times would last,
But that's the folly of the past—
Now Paradise is burning.

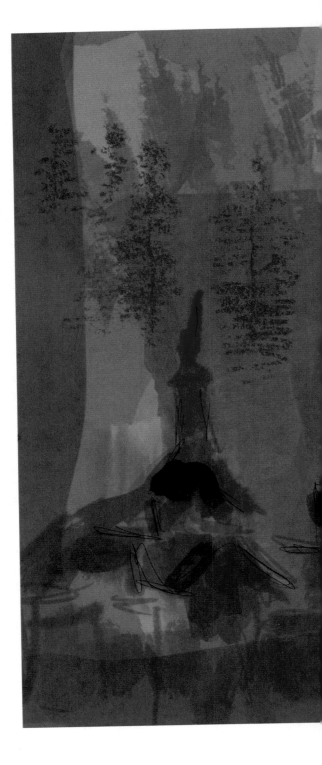

Paradise is Burning

In November of 2018, the most destructive wildfire in California history known as The Camp Fire swallowed the town of Paradise. It was the deadliest fire in the United States since 1918. Eighty-six people lost their lives and the town of Paradise, home to 26,000 residents, was completely consumed. The tragedy was definitively linked to global climate change and heralded as the beginning of many more such fires predicted to ravage the western United States in years to come.

Agree Box—Check

Follow me, follow me, where'er I roam,
Know my location through my telephone.
I give permission
For face recognition
And twenty-four seven surveillance by drone.

To Zuckerburg, Bezos, Google and Mac,
I grant free use of the data you track.
To access your sites,
My privacy rights
And personal life you may evermore hack.

Know my relationships outside and in,
Know my financials and all that I spend.
I'm certain you'll tell me
If ever you sell me—
I trust you Big Brotherly billionaire friend.

Agree Box—Check
Privacy rights and protections have been outpaced by technological innovation. The simple act of checking *I agree to these terms* often means relinquishing privacy rights in ways that were once unthinkable— from online searches, purchases, and financial records, to our most intimate communications, medical information, and whereabouts at all times. This data is often sold to marketing companies without our clear consent, while outdated privacy laws and a growing surveillance apparatus allow the government to monitor Americans like never before.

Huckabee Huckabee Hullabaloo

Huckabee, Huckabee, Hullabaloo
Went down to the press corps
With one thing to do.
Whatever the president said
We all knew,
Huckabee'd share it and swear it was true.

She'd coolly legitimize acts of the POTUS
And spin altered facts
from the fibs that she'd quote us,
While claiming the *media's* stories
Weren't true!
Huckabee, Huckabee, Hullabaloo.

Huckabee, Huckabee, Hullaballoo
Sarah Huckabee Sanders served as White House Press Secretary under President Trump from July, 2017- 2019, making her only the third woman in U.S. history to hold that position. The Mueller Report, released in April of 2019, noted that Sanders admitted to investigators under oath that she had made false statements to the public as press secretary. Known for deftly supporting the president by validating his remarks and nefarious actions, she once stated, "I can definitively say the president is not a liar, and I think it's frankly insulting that question would be asked."

There was a Crooked Man

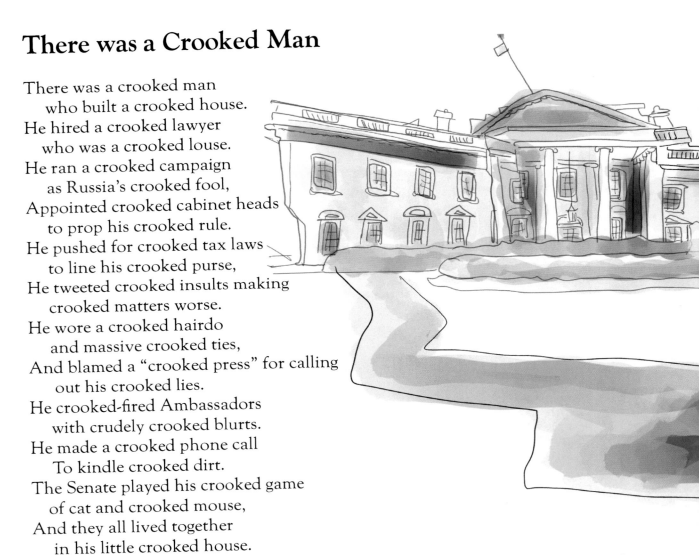

There was a crooked man
    who built a crooked house.
He hired a crooked lawyer
    who was a crooked louse.
He ran a crooked campaign
    as Russia's crooked fool,
Appointed crooked cabinet heads
    to prop his crooked rule.
He pushed for crooked tax laws
    to line his crooked purse,
He tweeted crooked insults making
    crooked matters worse.
He wore a crooked hairdo
    and massive crooked ties,
And blamed a "crooked press" for calling
    out his crooked lies.
He crooked-fired Ambassadors
    with crudely crooked blurts.
He made a crooked phone call
    To kindle crooked dirt.
The Senate played his crooked game
    of cat and crooked mouse,
And they all lived together
    in his little crooked house.

After *There Was a Crooked Man,* The Mother Goose Nursery Rhymes

There Was a Crooked Man

President Donald Trump is considered "crooked" by many Americans and others throughout the world. Numerous lawsuits have plagued his political and business careers leading to dozens of financial settlements, counter-lawsuits, and even impeachment by the House of Representatives in 2019. While in the White House, a host of Mr. Trump's associates have been convicted of crimes including his Campaign Chairman, National Security Advisor, personal attorney, and multiple friends, advisors, and fixers. Dozens of others have been charged with crimes both in the U.S. and in Russia.

Acquit Me in the Springtime

Acquit me in the springtime
As trees begin to bloom,
When all is well in Washington
And warblers start to croon.
When fields are clothed with splendor
In gowns of grassy green.
Acquit me in the springtime
When all the world's serene.

Endorse my crude behaviors
And lawless acts of rule,
Break oaths of Constitution
Fine senators—you *fools!*
While bees are making honey,
While sap is on the rise,
Acquit me in the springtime
And compromise your lives.

My Twitter-tweets, like birdsong
Will fill the air each hour,
As you bestow upon me
Sweet unimpeded power.
No heads need pike-impalement
Lest you step out of line!
Acquit me in the springtime
And all the world is *Mine.*

Acquit Me in the Springtime
President Donald Trump was tried for Abuse of Power and Obstruction of Congress in a highly irregular Senate Impeachment trial in early 2020. Absurdly, almost every senator agreed privately that the president was actually guilty as charged—but a majority were afraid to convict him, lest they face retribution from Mr. Trump and his supporters. Senate Majority Leader Mitch McConnell orchestrated the political show culminating in a mostly partisan acquittal, handing the president virtually unlimited power and diminishing the balance of powers set forth in the Constitution.

Remember the Days When News Was Real?

A major shift in the way we get our news has brought with it the constant need to question the veracity of what we read, see, and hear. With the increased predominance of streaming news sources, the demise of hundreds of printed newspapers, and a trend towards "entertainment news," there has been a marked decline in investigative journalism, and a rise in openly biased news outlets. During the 2016 election cycle, it became evident that false stories were being published to bolster clickbait ad revenues and to influence voter groups with sensational falsehoods. Making matters worse, President Trump began to claim that accurate, well-sourced stories were fake, further muddying the nation's confidence in factual news reporting.

Remember the Days
When News was Real?

Remember the days when news was real,
Reporters were urged to dig into the deal,
When there was no clickbait to pass on fake news,
And no one was spoon-fed their personal views?

Remember when there were no pundits around,
The omniscient experts employed to expound
On all-day news channels that only inflame,
While breaking news banners befuddle our brains?

Remember when Facebook seemed sort of cute,
You could keep up with friends and like them to boot;
No Russians or trolls posted toxic selections
To influence culture or throw our elections?

Remember the paper that came to the door
With in-depth reporting of stories, and more—
How we'd ponder and think and discuss what we read
And disagree kindly with what others said?

Remember Democracy wasn't so wrecked
When journalists managed to keep it in check,
When leaders were statesmen who did more than schmooze,
And political figures did not cry *fake news?*

Made in the USA
Coppell, TX
05 October 2020